Living Relationships

Lesley Husselbee

NATIONAL CHRISTIAN EDUCATION COUNCIL

Other worship resources published by NCEC

Celebrating Series . . .

A series of six books for all-age festival services:
Celebrating Christmas Books 1 & 2
Celebrating Lent & Easter Books 1 & 2
Celebrating Harvest
Celebrating Special Sundays

Anthologies of material for private reflection and public worship

A Word in Season
Liturgy of Life
Flowing Streams
Prayers for the Church Community

Cover design: Julian Smith
Cover photo: Ffotograff, Cardiff

Published by:
National Christian Education Council
Robert Denholm House
Nutfield
Redhill RH1 4HW

British Library Cataloguing-in-publication Data:
A catalogue record for this book is available
from the British Library.

ISBN 0-7197-0826-5

First published 1994
© 1994 Lesley Husselbee

Typeset by Avonset, Midsomer Norton, nr. Bath
Printed in Great Britain by
Clifford Frost Ltd., Wimbledon, London

CONTENTS

FOREWORD TO THE SERIES

This is the fourth in a series of six books which offer services of worship for all ages in the church. The details of the other five can be found on the back cover of the book. The authors write from a wide experience of leading all-age worship and the *Living Worship* . . . series springs from that experience.

In the celebration of Christian worship every age group has something to contribute. The experiences of each member of the congregation, regardless of age, can be used, and should be valued. The ability and willingness of children to enter into a wide range of worship experiences should not be underestimated. Adults should be encouraged to accept the gifts which children bring to worship.

There is no 'audience' in all-age worship. The children are not performing for the adults; neither are they passive spectators to adult worship. These services provide the means by which the whole church family can engage in its most important responsibility and joy: the worship of God through Jesus Christ.

These books will serve churches best when a group of people, representative of all ages in the church meet to plan the worship, and are prepared to give time and thought to the preparation. Those who use them should feel free to adapt them to the needs of the local church community. In any one church they may well emerge on a Sunday morning looking quite different from the details given on the printed pages that follow.

Unless the flow of the service requires it, no place is given for either the Lord's Prayer, the offertory or announcements. These should be included according to local practice.

Donald Hilton
Series Editor

PREFACE

Human relationships aren't always easy. The Bible has many stories showing us how best to create good human relationships, but it also offers examples of broken relationships, disturbed family life, and disharmony in national and international relationships. However, the honesty of the description of broken relationships in the Bible stories never obscures the biblical vision of a world of living human relationships that inspire peace and joy. It constantly affirms that this is God's ultimate intention for us all.

This series of four services recognizes the difficulties and tensions of human relationships. The first service explores the way in which each of our lives can be enriched by working together and sharing in community. The second celebrates the value of our differences, while the third struggles to find ways in which we can use conflict creatively rather than destructively. The final service, which could be used as an anniversary service, remembers the saints of the past and rejoices in the saints of today. It defines 'saint' in the biblical sense of 'those who love God'. Throughout all the services there is the challenge to us all in our personal relationships to go on growing more like Christ.

Lesley Husselbee

5

TOGETHERNESS

A service to celebrate Christian community

Introduction

This service explores human interdependence and the way in which a sense of community is more satisfying than independence, and more effective than solitariness. In fact, no-one can live in isolation; by our very nature as human beings, we need each other. Even those who, by choice or necessity spend much time alone depend on others. However, care must be taken in this service to express this interdependence in a way that does not alienate those who feel themselves to be deprived of companionship.

Preparation

Collect and display around the church as many patchwork articles as possible, showing by their design how small pieces of material can be brought together to make a pattern that is more pleasing than any one piece of the material could be.

Make a template of a hexagon (say 10-20cm in length and depth), large enough to be recognized from the back of the church when it is used at the front, and produce sufficient hexagons from it to make the pattern you decide upon (see later instructions and diagram on page 42 which uses 73 hexagons). Try to ensure that every member of the congregation has at least one. Cut the hexagons from two kinds of card:

1) Patterned cards e.g. by using old Christmas cards or wallpaper glued to thin card. (The design on page 42 requires 24 patterned shapes.)

2) Single coloured thin card. (the design on page 42 requires 49 single coloured shapes.)

Mark the back of each shape with either a 'P' for the patterned hexagon, or 'C' for a coloured hexagon. Attach a small piece of Blu-tack onto the back of each shape. Prepare a large board to receive the shapes, marking the hexagons on the board with the equivalent 'P' or 'C'. Either design your own interlocking pattern or use the design on page 43.

Prepare Ruth 1.1-18 dramatically and Acts 2.43-47 as a choral reading for three people.
You will need a loaf of bread.
Invite six people to play the parts of BAKER, FARMER etc., and prepare the labels to go round their necks.

ORDER OF SERVICE

As people arrive give them one or more of the hexagons that will be used to make the pattern.

Opening worship

Call to worship

Invite the congregation to look around and identify people they know very well indeed, others who are less well known to them, and also those they hardly know at all. Ask them to keep those thoughts in mind throughout the service. Introduce the versicle and response to the opening prayer.

To the Leader's words: How wonderful it is, how pleasant.
invite the response **for God's people to live together in harmony!**

Psalm 133.1 (GNB)

READER   As long age as the 17th century John Donne reminded us: 'No man is an island, entire of itself; every man is a piece of the continent, a part of the main; if a clod be washed away by the sea, Europe is the less, as well as if a promontory were, as well as if a manor of thy friends were. Any man's death diminishes me, because I am involved in mankind. And therefore never send to know for whom the bell tolls; it tolls for thee.'

LEADER   How wonderful it is, how pleasant

RESPONSE   **for God's people to live together in harmony!**

READER   In our own century J B Priestley reminded us: 'We don't live alone. We are members of one body. We are responsible for each other, and I tell you that the time will soon come when, if (we) will not learn that lesson, then, (we) will be taught it in fire and blood and anguish.'

from An Inspector Calls

8

LEADER	How wonderful it is, how pleasant
RESPONSE	**for God's people to live together in harmony!**
READER	We who are united with Christ, though many, form one body, and belong to one another as its limbs and organs.
LEADER	How wonderful it is, how pleasant
RESPONSE	**for God's people to live together in harmony!**

Hymn   'As we are gathered'
       or 'For the beauty of the earth'

Prayers

We remember that Christ is with us.
Lord, we are your people.
You have gathered us together
to share in your purpose
and advance your kingdom
of love, justice and peace.
In our worship and devotion
open our minds to know your will.

Kate Johnson

We confess that we have often damaged the Christian community.
If we have been hurt by something said to us;
if we feel we have been treated unfairly;
if someone else has been chosen when we had hoped to be;
help us not to nurse a grievance about it.

If we have tried to be helpful and no-one has thanked us;
if we have put ourselves out and no-one has noticed;
if we did our best but were told we had failed;
help us not to nurse a grievance about it.

If we told the truth and were not believed;
if we have been let down by someone we trusted;
if we have supported a good cause but failed to win support;
help us not to nurse a grievance about it.

It is so easy, Lord, to be bitter about these things, and to stop trying. Give us a spirit like yours, so that we refuse to be put off or discouraged.

from *Prayers for the Church Community*

In praise of togetherness

Story:
On 29th May, 1953, Edmund Hillary and Sherpa Tensing eventually reached the top of Mount Everest. They were the first people ever to stand on the summit of the highest place on earth, with the whole world stretching out below them in every direction. Hillary wrote later of that very special moment like this:

> 'I looked at Tensing. In spite of the balaclava helmet, goggles and oxygen mask – all encrusted with icicles – that concealed his face, there was no disguising his grin of delight as he looked all around him. We shook hands, and then Tensing threw his arm around my shoulders and we thumped each other on the back until we were almost breathless. It was 11.30am.'

It had been a hard, strenuous climb, and had only been achieved by teamwork. Sir John Hunt, leader of the expedition, wrote:

> 'The greatness of climbing on the highest hills lies in the fact that no single man is capable of reaching a summit by his own efforts.'

from *The Ascent of Everest* by John Hunt

Hillary and Tensing were only able to reach the 'top of the world' because they were part of a great team of many mountaineers, porters, administrators and caterers.

In our lives, there are many mountains to climb, and the path may seem difficult at times. It's wonderful when we triumph. But it is important to say, at those times, not 'Look what I have done', but 'Look what I have been able to do through the help of other people, and God'.

Invite the congregation to look at the hexagon(s) they were given as they arrived. Draw attention to the different types. Each one is colourful itself, but the six edges are almost asking to be joined to others. One hexagon doesn't look much by itself, but the patchwork articles around the church suggest that if each hexagon was put with others it might become something more significant.

During the following activity a small choir sings:
  'Jesu, Jesu, fill us with your love'
  or 'Bind us together'
  or 'God is love, his the care'
Ask the congregation to bring up their hexagons. Let them stick the patterned hexagons on the places on the board marked with a 'P' and the plain coloured hexagons on the places on the board marked with a 'C'. Guide people as necessary to ensure that the overall pattern emerges on the board. As this is done comment on the way in which the value of each piece is not only recognized but increased as the hexagons come together. Two plus two somehow equals more than four!

Bible readings

1) Ruth 1.1-18
   Tell this in as dramatic a way as possible. There is a version in the Dramatised Bible page 203. Alternatively, turn it into a short play, or mime it as it is read from the Bible.

2) Acts 2.43-47
   Present this as a choral reading in the following way, using the Good News Bible. The 'echoes' should be people with good carrying voices, and be standing in different parts of the church, perhaps unseen by the congregation.

NARRATOR	Many miracles and wonders were being done through the apostles, and everyone was filled with awe. All the believers continued together in close fellowship
FIRST ECHO	in close fellowship
SECOND ECHO	close fellowship
NARRATOR	and shared their belongings with one another.
FIRST ECHO	shared their belongings with one another.
SECOND ECHO	their belongings with one another
NARRATOR	They would sell their property and possessions,
FIRST ECHO	They would sell their property and possessions,
SECOND ECHO	their property and possessions,
NARRATOR	and distribute the money among all,
FIRST ECHO	distribute the money among all,
SECOND ECHO	money among all,
NARRATOR	according to what each one needed. Day

11

	after day they met as a group in the Temple, and they had their meals together in their homes,
FIRST ECHO	meals together in their homes,
SECOND ECHO	together in their homes,
NARRATOR	eating with glad and humble hearts, praising God, and enjoying the good will of all the people. And every day the Lord added to the group those who were being saved.
FIRST ECHO	being saved.
SECOND ECHO	being saved.

Hymn   'I come with joy to meet my Lord'
or 'The church is like a table'
or 'Help us to help each other, Lord'

Together in order to share

Bible reading   Luke 14.15-24 (The Great Feast)

Comment
The man holding the party, or feast, couldn't have held it by himself. Whoever heard of a one person party! First, he invited 'VIP' guests – the socially acceptable people, but they refused to come to the party for one reason or another. Then he invited all the so-called 'riff raff' – the socially unacceptable people – to come instead. They jumped at the chance and had a very good time! The first people he invited had rejected the spirit of community, so the host created a new and different community. But of course, the parable isn't about parties in the usual sense. The host is God and he is inviting us into the kingdom of heaven – the best party there ever was! He wants us to join together as Christians, because, in doing this we can share our love for one another, enjoy being together, and support one another. Of course, like the 'VIP' guests in the parable, we can refuse to come to the party, but if so we miss out on a great deal. That saddens God, though he will never be short of guests.

In the parable the host invited anyone and everyone. He didn't say, 'I just want to invite this little group of people because we get on so well together'. He took the risk of inviting the most unlikely people. The Church must take the same sort of risk and invite everyone to our worship, church groups and clubs.

Celebration

Produce a loaf of bread and put it on a table where everyone can see it. Various people wearing large placards (BAKER, LORRY DRIVER etc.) round their necks now come to the front of the church, offer a brief comment and exit. Remember that all jobs are open to men and women.

BAKER	Good morning! I'm the baker who baked that bread. I'm just on my way to the firm who supplies my yeast. I couldn't manage without it.
MILLER	Hello! I'm the miller who provided the baker with the flour that went into the bread. Can't stop now. I'm on my way to the farmer to order my next supply of wheat. No wheat, no flour No flour, no bread.
FARMER	How do y'do! I'm the farmer who grew the wheat that the baker used. Forgive me if I rush. I've got to telephone the engineer. My tractor needs a service. I've got fields to plough for next year's wheat.
ACCOUNTANT	Hello! Nice to see you all! Wish I could stay *(looks at watch)*, but I've promised to meet a farmer who's got behind with his accounts. Then there's a chap from a big milling company who wants to talk about his VAT.
DRIVER	Hey! Tell me please – is there a garage near here? I'm running short of diesel oil. I've got a massive load of flour for some baker, and then later today I'm delivering fertilizer to a farmer a couple of miles away. Oh, there it is. *(He points)* I can see it. Thanks! Sorry, can't stay. Must rush.
SHOP ASSISTANT	*(Looking at watch)* Is it that late? Nice chap my boss – the baker round the corner, you know. But he does like me to get to work on time. Quite right too, I suppose. We get long queues at our shop. All home-made, you know. You should try some.

Cut the loaf into smaller sections and pass it round the congregation for each person to break a piece and eat. Use the following poem against a background of music as they do so.

Poem

Back of the loaf is the snowy flour,
Back of the flour, the mill,
Back of the mill, the sun, the shower,
The wind, and our Father's will.
Back of all food is human toil,
Back of our toil, the skill,
Back of the skill, the call to all,
To further the Father's will.

(anon)

Comment

In Old Testament times, the way in which the community which received Ruth showed that they accepted her, was to allow her to glean from their corn fields. They shared their bread with her. The early community of Christians also shared their bread with one another. Being a Christian is being a member of a community, sharing with one another, and caring for each other. Eating together is one of the many ways in which we show our togetherness.

Invite the congregation to look around again and, choosing those people they know less well, decide who they will speak to after the service.

Prayer

Loving God, you have placed us in a world where we depend
very much on each other. We thank you for the many people
who work to make our lives more comfortable and enjoyable.
We remember with gratitude
    those who collect our rubbish,
    those who deliver our post,
    and those who provide public transport.
We thank you
    for those who provide us with fuel to warm our homes,
    for those who work in schools, surgeries and hospitals.
Help us Father, so that we may
    listen to those around us and better appreciate strangers,
    share with people who come from a different race, or
    appreciate and work with people who are not immediately
    attractive to us.
In silence, we pray for the people sitting near us
    and for the whole community of this church,

for the community of this town/village
and the places in the world where the sense of community has
broken down.
We offer these prayers in the name of Jesus who created a
community of disciples, and gave us a hope of new community
that will touch all nations and people.

Hymn   'There's a spirit in the air'

Benediction
Go in peace to serve the Lord, confident that all in heaven and on
earth is to be brought into a unity in Christ; and the blessing of God
Almighty, the Father, the Son and the Holy Spirit be with you always.
Amen

ENJOY THE DIFFERENCE!

Introduction
This service celebrates the variety of God's creation of which we are a part.

Preparation
Invite several families or groups in the church to prepare table or poster exhibitions to show the variety of God's creation. The themes chosen will depend on the time of year, but might include a variety of flowers, either in single vases or made into an arrangement; a collection of green or dried leaves pasted to a board; pictures of trees, animals or birds; a collection of cloud pictures.

Choose one of the two suggestions on pages 20 & 21 which aim to remind the congregation how boring uniformity can be. The first is about identical human 'clones', the second about a boring meal.

If you select the 'cloning' suggestion, make six identical large photocopies (say, A3 size) of a photograph of a particular person; preferably someone unknown to the congregation.

If you select the 'boring meal', prepare a large, imposing menu thus:

Starter
Bread, Butter and Cheese

Main Course
Cheese, Bread and Butter

Dessert
Bread, Cheese and Butter

with biscuits and cheese to follow

Prepare a table with tablecloth, napkins and glasses.
Prepare the two sketches based on 1 Corinthians 12.12-31. Ensure that the people taking part can be seen and heard. For the second sketch

you will need silhouettes of parts of the body, and a board to stick them onto.

ORDER OF SERVICE

Call to worship
> Let all the earth acclaim the Lord!
> Worship the Lord in gladness;
> enter his presence with joyful song.
> Acknowledge that the Lord is God;
> he made us and we are his,
> his own people, the flock which he shepherds.
> Enter his gates with thanksgiving,
> his courts with praise.
> Give thanks to him and bless his name;
> for the Lord is good and his love is everlasting,
> his faithfulness endures to all generations.

Psalm 100 (REB)

Hymn   'All creatures of our God and King'
or 'To God who makes all lovely things'
or 'Immortal, invisible, God only wise'

Prayer (*use two voices*)

VOICE 1   Glorious Lord, we give you greeting!
VOICE 2   Let the church and chancel praise you,
Let the plain and hillside praise you,
Let the world's three well-springs praise you,
Let the dark and the daylight praise you.
VOICE 1   Abraham, founder of the faith praised you:
Let the life everlasting praise you,
Let the birds and the honeybees praise you,
Let the shorn stems and the shoots praise you.
VOICE 2   Both Aaron and Moses praised you:
Let the male and the female praise you,
Let the seven days and the stars praise you,
Let the air and the ether praise you,
Let the fish in the swift seas praise you,
Let the thought and the action praise you,
Let all the good that's performed praise you.

17

VOICE 1   And I shall praise you, Lord of glory;
           Glorious Lord, I give you greeting!

Anonymous Welsh prayer

Enjoying difference

Either, display the six identical photocopies one by one:
    'This is one person in the world.'
    'And this is another!'
    'Here's another person!'; and so on through the six identical people.
Comment that no matter how attractive, clever, humorous or brilliant such a person was, we would soon be bored with a world full of identical people.
Or, invite selected members of the congregation to share in a meal. Seat them at the prepared table. Call on a suitably dressed waiter and ask the diners what they would like to eat at a big celebratory meal. To every suggestion they make tell them, 'I'm afraid that's off the menu today, but we have got plenty of other things to eat'. Eventually, produce your large, imposing menu:

Starter
Bread, Butter and Cheese

Main Course
Cheese, Bread and Butter

Dessert
Bread, Cheese and Butter

with biscuits and cheese to follow

Despite the best attentions of the waiter, the guests, suitably prepared beforehand, should comment on the boring nature of the meal and demand variety. After a while, they return to their seats, one of them loudly remarking, 'Never mind, come home with me. We can have a cheese sandwich!'

Comment

But take care! There's a danger of something like that happening to us. Sometimes planners, bureaucrats and politicians seem to welcome a world of identical people who fit into identical box-homes, eat identical food, wear identical clothes, and accept identical black and white facts from identical tabloid newspapers. Adolf Hitler wanted to create the perfect race of blonde, white Arians, and the extermination of anyone who failed to fit into his neat plan.

Advertisers seem to live in a stereo-typed world of slim, young couples with perfect complexions, who live on mass-produced and identical microwave-able diet meals, and then drive around in identical cars, having first removed all human body odours by identical deodorants. They give birth to 2.4 children who play with identical serial toys from which the producers make vast inflated profits.

We'll resist them! Let us celebrate our differences, and enjoy them! This is how God made us!

God's world of variety
According to the table or poster exhibitions that are displayed around the church, explore the great variety of God's creation. Ensure that everyone can see the exhibits either by inviting people to the tables, or parading the posters around the church. Play suitable music such as Vivaldi's 'The Four Seasons', as you do so.

The variety of human nature
Explore the variety within the congregation. Ask people to stand if:

* *they have:*

blue eyes	grey eyes	brown eyes	some other colour
fair hair	brown hair	auburn hair	grey hair

* *they would prefer a holiday in:*

America	Europe	India	China

* *they would sooner listen to:*

Radio 1	Radio 2	Radio 3	Radio 4
Radio 5	Classic FM	Their local Radio Station	

* *their favourite colour is:*

red	blue	green	pink	brown etc.

* *they came to church first as a:*

child	teenager	pensioner	another age

Comment

We are all different, as different as God intended us to be. The one thing that is the same about us all is that God made us, and loves us.

Hymn   'God is love, his the care'
           or 'Many are the lightbeams from the one light'

Difference is useful

Use the sketch(es) based on 1 Corinthians 12. If time is short use only one, but where possible use them both with a quietly sung verse or chorus in between. Where possible learn the scripts.

Sketch 1

Those taking part are a minister (or vicar, priest etc.), church leader (elder, deacon, class steward, church warden etc.), two church members, a child, and a narrator. They should wear large labels around their necks, or some item of clothing or an object to show who they are: e.g. dog collar for the minister, toy for the child, minute book for the leader.

NARRATOR	Welcome to our church. Please meet our happy Christian community.
MINISTER	I'm the minister. *(Points to dog collar)* I'm the most important person here. I'm employed by the church, and I know more about the Bible than anyone else. I went to theological college for five years!
LEADER	*(Elbowing the Minister away)* Ministers? They come and go. Some of us have been here since we were children. In any case, you wouldn't do very well on your own. It's the (elders) who actually run things and make decisions. You couldn't do without us!
FIRST MEMBER	*(Elbowing Leader from central position)* But it wouldn't be much of a church with just chiefs and no Indians. It's people like me who are the real church. Just see what would happen if we all stayed away one week. We keep the church going. We make the tea, we arrange the flowers, sing and *(add local examples)* We are the church!

20

CHILD	*(Jumping into the central position)* You're all wrong. It's children who are more important than anyone. We are the future church. And anyway the Bible says that the Kingdom of heaven belongs to us. Anyway, *(hesitantly)* I think it does.
FIRST MEMBER	*(Taking the child by the arm and removing him/her)* What rubbish! You're not important. You are too young. You don't understand yet! Seen and not heard. that's what I say about children.
SECOND MEMBER	*(Joining the others)* I don't know what you're all arguing about. At least we all come to church. It's those wicked people outside that I blame. They are the sinners! We are obviously better than they are!

The rest of the sketch will need to be written in the light of local experience and matching the actual experience of the local church.

NARRATOR	*(Gently leading the other characters away)* I have the feeling that we've not got it quite right. They seem to know that they are all different, but not how to use their differences in the right way. Let's try again. Now calm down everyone! Think about it and lets see if we want to put it differently. *(They all confer, heads together and move slightly to one side)*
MINISTER	*(Quietly stepping to a central position, and bringing a child with him/her)* Please meet, *(Name the child)* He's been coming to our church for two years now. He means a lot to us. Some of us older ones find computers difficult to get on with, but he's a whizz-kid with them and has helped a lot of us. *(The skill should be changed to fit the reality of the actual child in the sketch)*
CHILD	*(Fetching FIRST MEMBER)* But that only happened because I was invited out to tea with some other boys and girls in the church.

21

	This was the family we went to. They were very kind to us.
FIRST MEMBER	That all came out of a Church Family Day we held. We talked about how we could encourage a spirit of care in this church and one idea was to try and build bridges across the age-groups. Members of the Women's Meeting visited the Youth Club, the Cub Scouts put on a party for older people and, at Cub Scouts I met. *(Name the child)*. It went on from there.
LEADER	We were doing Bible study when that idea first occurred to us. You know, where Paul says the church is like a body. We are all different, but our differences are good and can help us to grow. What's the use of an arm without a head, or a foot without an eye. We all need each other.
SECOND MEMBER	*(Stepping forward)* And it all changes. Sometimes one person is the thinker – the head- with ideas, and others are the arms doing the practical work. Then it all changes and the arm becomes a head and the foot turns out to be a hand after all. If you see what I mean. *(They all laugh)*
NARRATOR	reads Romans 12.6-8

Chorus   'Ubi caritas et amor'
          or 'Laudate omni gentes'
          or some other short verse.

Second sketch
Plan characters to represent parts of the human body: the head, arms, legs, torso etc. Each one carries or wears a silhouette outline of the appropriate part of the body. These will be stuck onto a board with Blu-tack to make a complete picture of the body.

They walk around the church fastening the silhouettes to various pieces of church furniture e.g. the lectern, a wall, the pulpit, but are clearly dissatisfied with the result. Slowly they all converge on one place and, after much trial and error, fit them all together to form a body. As the body is formed, the Bible is read.

Reading   1 Corinthians 12.14-20

Hymn   'As we are gathered, Jesus is here';
           or 'God is love, and where true love is'
           or 'Brother, sister, let me serve you'

Comment

We all have a variety of talents which we can use to share with one another. God has given us so many gifts and wants us to use them all. For example, the first disciples were all different. Think how their differences were used by God!

God needs all of us; in all of our variety, however little we, or others may value them. He can use us.

Meditation

Encourage the congregation to think about the variety of gifts that each one of them has, and ask how as a community they could each offer those talents.

Hymn   'We are your people, Lord'

Prayer *(use several voices. Invite the congregation to use the response)*
Dear Lord, fill your church with love and understanding, so that we may show your gospel love.
    In your name we pray.
Fill your people with respect for each other, a willingness to listen and a generosity to share.
    In your name we pray.
Enable us to listen to and help all who suffer through injustice and neglect.
    In your name we pray.
May those with skill and understanding, with knowledge and intellect be so guided by your love,that they harness their power for the good of all.
    In your name we pray.
May those who suffer in pain, distress, loneliness and grief know the power of your healing love, through human companionship.
    In your name we pray.
May we, in all we do and say, in all we are and strive to be, be filled with your loving power.
    In your name we pray.

Anne Knighton

Hymn   'I come with joy to meet my Lord'

Blessing *(Said together)*
The grace of our Lord Jesus Christ, and the love of God, and the
fellowship of the Holy Spirit be with us all evermore. Amen

HANDLING CONFLICT

Introduction

In reconciling humanity to God, Jesus Christ gave resources to his people to become a reconciling Church. Within a relatively short period of time the early Church took steps to heal the ancient divisions between Jews and Gentiles, and affirmed that 'in Christ there is no such thing as Jew and Greek, slave and freeman, male and female; for you are all one person in Christ Jesus.'

Even so the Acts of the Apostles record strong disagreement among Christians. Paul's letters expose violent arguments in the early Church. The Church today is similarly ambivalent. It is the healer of conflict, yet sometimes the cause of conflict. This service acknowledges the ambivalence with confession, and affirms the positive ways available to us to handle conflict creatively. In particular it challenges us by making us aware of the ways in which Jesus dealt with conflict.

Preparation

Obtain the poster, 'Two mules - a Fable for the Nations', published by Quaker Peace and Service. Poster available from Friends Book Centre, Friends House, Euston Road, London NW1 2BJ, or enlarge the one given on page 45.

Set up two chairs about five metres apart at the front of the church. Place a few sweets on each chair. Obtain a three metre length of cord to tie two people together for the first item of the service. Plan how this will be done with safety e.g. the two people should be of roughly equal size and strength, and wear a strong belt to which the cord can be attached. Rehearse the action well before the service.

Prepare the drama which presents the Mark 11.15-19 reading and/or find several readers to read the dramatic version of Mark 14.53-65. Find readers for the prayers of intercession.

If you are following the suggestion given on page 29, prepare pieces of paper which will be given to the congregation before the service. Find a fireproof container to collect these.

ORDER OF SERVICE

Call to worship
Jesus said:'You have heard that they were told, 'Love your neighbour and hate your enemy.' But what I tell you is this: Love your enemies and pray for your persecutors; only so can you be children of your heavenly Father, who causes the sun to rise on good and bad alike, and sends the rain on the innocent and the wicked.

Matthew 5.43-45 (REB)

Hymn   'O love of God, how strong and true'

Prayer
Our loving Father, and Father of ALL
We thank you for having brought us together
in this land to learn to love you
and one another.

We thank you for our Church with
its diverse membership.
We know, Gracious Father, that we have
not always been obedient to you.

Give us courage, we pray, to stand up
for your truth.

Make us apostles of your love, justice,
hope, reconciliation and peace.

We ask all this in his name,
the Prince of Peace,
our Lord and Master, Jesus Christ.

Stanley Mogoba

The Two Donkeys
The two people will have rehearsed the drama based on the Quaker poster, but they should seek to make it look spontaneous as first of all they pull each other from one side to the other, greedy for the sweets. Then they pause, think, confer with each other, and move first to one chair to eat one set of sweets, and then to the other. Show the congregation the picture of the two donkeys.

Comment

When confrontation gives way to co-operation everyone is satisfied. There is a good deal of conflict in human lives; some of it obvious and some hidden. Newspapers and television offer evidence enough. *(mention recent examples)* Most of the soaps and plays that we watch on television involve conflict of one kind or another. *(Give examples)* Conflict also arises in our own family life, at work and in the church. How does conflict arise? Is it because humanity is so varied and thus our differences create problems? Is most conflict due to greed and selfishness? Should we seek to avoid all conflict? Is there a way of handling conflict creatively and thus turn something that can easily be destructive into something creative?

Jesus told us to 'turn the other cheek' when people insult us. Does this mean that we are to become mere doormats, allowing anything to happen so that there can be perpetual peace and quiet; or does it mean that we sometimes have to face up to conflict; even initiate conflict, in order that justice can be done?

Let's see how Jesus handled conflict, and always matched his solution to the particular circumstances of the moment.

Jesus Confronted Conflict

Sometimes Jesus firmly stood for those who were being exploited and oppressed by the powerful. Do you remember the story of the money-changers in the temple?

Bible reading   Mark 11.15-19
Act out this reading as someone slowly reads the story. Actors should mime the various characters e.g. Jesus, the money-changers, people holding cardboard cut-out doves and sheep, the Pharisees.

Hymn   'We pray for peace, but not the easy peace'
        or 'Eternal Ruler of the ceaseless round' (verses 1, 3, 4)

Jesus was silent in the face of conflict

Bible reading   Mark 14.53-65
Use the following dramatic version of the reading:

NARRATOR   Then Jesus was taken to the High Priest's
                             house, where all the chief priests, the leaders,
                             and the teachers of the Law were gathering.

Peter followed from a distance and went into the courtyard of the High Priest's house. There he sat down with the guards, keeping himself warm by the fire. The chief priests and the whole Council tried to find some evidence against Jesus in order to put him to death. But they could not find any. Many witnesses told lies against Jesus, but their stories did not agree. Then some men stood up and told this lie against Jesus:

WITNESS We heard him say, 'I will tear down this Temple which men have made, and after three days I will build one that is not made by men.'

NARRATOR Not even they, however, could make their stories agree. The High Priest stood up in front of them all and questioned Jesus.

HIGH PRIEST Have you no answer to the accusation they bring against you?

NARRATOR But Jesus kept quiet and would not say a word. Again the High Priest questioned him.

HIGH PRIEST Are you the Messiah, the Son of the Blessed God?

NARRATOR Jesus answered:

JESUS I am, and you will see the Son of Man seated on the right of the Almighty and coming with the clouds of heaven!

NARRATOR The High Priest tore his robes and said,

HIGH PRIEST We don't need any more witnesses! You heard his blasphemy. What is your decision?

NARRATOR They all voted against him; he was guilty and should be put to death. Some of them began to spit upon Jesus, and they blindfolded him and hit him.

WITNESS Guess who hit you!

NARRATOR they said. And the guards took him and slapped him.

Sometimes Jesus absorbed violence

Bible reading   Mark 15.22-32

Hymn   'When I survey the wondrous cross'

Comment
So, Jesus handled conflict in different ways:
>   sometimes he confronted what was wrong;
>   sometimes he was silent;
>   sometimes he absorbed violence.

How are we to decide what to do? Let us first confess the times when we have brought about conflict in unhelpful ways:

Prayer of Confession
Either, on the small pieces of paper given to the congregation as they arrived, invite people to write the things they believe they have done that have hurt God or other people. Make it clear that this is between them and God. No-one else will ever see what they have written. Collect them in a fireproof container. Offer a prayer of confession and absolution. Set light to the prayers, or tear them up. Make it clear that this is a symbol of God's forgiveness. If they truly confessed, God had forgiven their sins before the papers were burnt. Then use the following prayer:

>   Eternal God,
>   Take fire, and burn our guilt and wrongdoing
>   Take water and wash our stained hands
>   Take love and cleanse our false and unloving hearts
>   Take our uncertain prayers and make them real and true so that
>   our desire for a new life meets your willing forgiveness and we
>   become free to serve you and each other.

Or, without the symbolism of burning paper, use the following prayer:

>   Dear God, what a mess we have made of your world, for always
>   we see one group set against another and oppression is like the
>   chorus in the human tragedy. We confess our part in this:
>   By silence, when we are too ignorant or too fearful to speak out.
>   By selfishness, when we pretend that all is well because we want
>   to keep our comfort.
>   By resignation, when we say that nothing can be done.

We ask for forgiveness. Change these sins within us, so that we may share in your saving work.

Bernard Thorogood

Hymn   'Make me a channel of your peace'
          or 'Jesus, Lord, we look to thee'

Can we be like Jesus?

Comment
No one answer.

Conflict was a part of Jesus' life. It is a part of our lives too. How do we deal with it? Do we run away from it? Or turn the other cheek? Do we confront evil, or seek to absorb the violence that conflict can create? Jesus handled violence, conflict and misunderstanding in different ways. With the money-changers in the temple, Jesus confronted injustice with physical anger. The money-changers were cheating and exploiting the poor in society and Jesus was angry at this exploitation. He didn't dodge the issue. He spoke out against the system which allowed them to cheat, and angrily turned over their tables. No-one was left in any doubt about what he thought, even though he must have known he was inviting violent retaliation against himself.

Sometimes Jesus was silent in the face of conflict. When he was arrested, he refused to struggle. Faced with the prodding questions of the High Priest, he kept silent. No self-defence; no anger. He accepted death on the cross. Had he retaliated he would have increased the violence to no good effect.

What are we to do when faced with conflict? Can we be like Jesus?

Reading
Use either of the following:
1. Kneeling on the ground,
    he made it clear that the Kingdom came
    not among the powerful, but the powerless;
    not through the wounders, but the wounded,
    not in the pleasure of the privileged,
    but in the pain of the rejected.

    Standing on his feet, he said that there was
    an alternative to greed   .   .   .   and that was sharing;

an alternative to apathy   .   .   .   and that was caring;
an alternative to violence   .   .   .   and that was getting
your face slapped
                      .   .   .   on both sides.
And on the cross   .   .   .
On the cross he pronounced God's last word
about what has to be done with criminals   .   .   .
They are to be loved and forgiven,
            loved and forgiven,
and that is the way the Kingdom comes.

John L. Bell & Graham Maule

2. The road Christ trod
    is not listed by the A.A.,
    or maintained by any highway authority.
    At best it is a footpath
    sometimes ploughed or blocked,
    and often it is painful
    to the feet.

    To tread it we must learn to be;
    So great that we can accept being nothing.
    So strong that we have no desire to inflict injury.
    So loving that we can endure hatred.
    So sure of the truth by which we live
    that we can bear to be called deceivers.
    So vitally alive that we are prepared when need be, to die.

Edmund Banyard

Hymn   'Put peace into each other's hands',
            or 'Help us to help each other, Lord'

Prayers of intercession *Use different readers from different age groups for each of the first three sections. The Leader should offer the rest of the prayer.*

Lord, we pray for those who are
the victims of conflict in the home:
For wives physically or verbally beaten,
For husbands who are made to feel small;
For children abused by adults,

31

For those who are not allowed to follow their own gifts.
We pray for broken families, and those affected by
constant rows.
Lord, heal their wounds.

Lord, we pray for those who are
the victims of conflict in our nation.
For those who are physically hurt or ignored
because they are of a different race, or age or social group.
We pray for those who stand up for the victims of abuse of
power, especially if it means that, like you, they are
misunderstood, or have to carry their cross.
Lord, heal their wounds.

Lord, we pray for the victims of conflict between nations
especially for the peoples of   .   .   .
We pray for the leaders of nations, for peace negotiators,
and all those who work for peace.
Lord, heal their wounds.

LEADER
Lord, it's always tempting to believe that when we became the
followers of Jesus we are spared the conflicts and tears of the
world; it's tempting too, to imagine that your Son Jesus has done
all the cross-carrying that is necessary.

Keep on reminding us that discipleship is about taking up new
crosses, that we are not protected from the cruelty of human
beings or the unanswerable circumstances of nature.

As Jesus our Lord was raised up in crucifixion, so lift up in our
lives those unusual qualities of meekness and unselfishness
·which the world derides as weak.
Bring glory to the lives lived in faithfulness to the truth, to
nations who seek justice and peace, and to your church where it
follows your way of suffering love.

Final sections by David Jenkins (adapted)

Hymn　　　'My song is love unknown

Comment
Jesus' example is a resource for us when we are faced with the possibility of conflict. But what effect can our little lives have on such big issues? Listen to a story.

Story: *The weight of a snowflake*
'Tell me the weight of a snowflake', a coalmouse asked a wild dove. 'Nothing more than nothing', was the answer. 'In that case, I must tell you a marvellous story', the coalmouse said. 'I sat on the branch of a fir, close to its trunk, when it began to snow – not heavily, not in a raging blizzard: no, just like a dream, without a sound and without any violence. Since I did not have anything better to do, I counted the snowflakes settling on the twigs and needles of my branch. Their number was exactly 3,741,952. When the 3,741,953rd dropped onto the branch – nothing more than nothing, as you say – the branch broke off.'

Having said that the coalmouse flew away. The dove, since Noah's time an authority on the matter, thought about the story for a while, and finally said to herself: 'Perhaps there is only one person's voice lacking for peace to come to the world.'

Kurt Kauter

Benediction
> The God of Peace will be with you
> and grant you peace at all times,
> peace beyond our understanding,
> that purifies the heart, mind and body,
> until his kingdom comes.

from South India

CALLED TO BE SAINTS

A service designed for an Anniversary

Introduction

This service thanks God for those who founded the local church and for all who have worshipped in it throughout its history. It seeks the guidance of the Holy Spirit for the future, so that the church might continue to serve God.

Preparation

Two or three weeks before the service, ask people to collect documents, photographs and other memorabilia of the church's history. Use these to make a large frieze to show the church's history. It will be most effective if the items can be displayed in chronological order so as to show the continuous life of the church community.

Well in advance of the service, invite members of the congregation to bring in a photograph of themselves. Alternatively, invite an all-age group to photograph people as they arrive in the weeks before the service is to be held. (Make sure you leave no-one out!) Turn these photographs into either a scrapbook, or preferably, a frieze (matching the historical frieze) in order to record the present membership.

Cut out enough triangular pennants, at least 20cm deep, so that each member of the congregation has one (see diagram). Put a hole in each of the corners of the short side of the triangle, and provide two wired plastic bag fasteners for each triangle or tie pieces of string or wool to each corner.

In advance of the service, invite five or six people to complete the

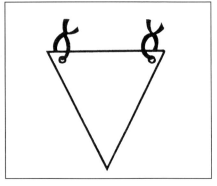

following sentence: 'I nominate *(name of person)* to be recognized as a saint because *(give reason).'* They will read their sentence during the service. Ask two members of the congregation to write personal prayers of mission and to be prepared to read them during the service.

Before the service begins tie string around pew end chairs, or pillars, or on canes readily accessible to the congregation, so that they can tie their pennants to the string during the service. Set three large candles in a conspicuous place and arrange for three people to light them at the appropriate moments. Plan to distribute small candles in protective card candle-holders. *(See diagram)*

Where possible plan two or three dramatic interludes to illustrate key times in the history of the local church. The call to worship will need to be duplicated for church use.

ORDER OF SERVICE

As people arrive give them a pennant and a small candle (unlit).

Call to worship

LEADER	Come to him as living stones, built up into a spiritual temple.
CONGREGATION	We are a holy priesthood offering spiritual sacrifice acceptable to God through Jesus Christ.
LEADER	You are a chosen race, a royal priesthood, a dedicated nation, a people claimed by God for his own
	Once you were not a people at all,
CONGREGATION	now we are God's people.
LEADER	Once you were outside his mercy,
CONGREGATION	now, we're no longer outside.
ALL	Thanks be to God through Jesus Christ.

adapted from 1 Peter 2.4-5, 9-10 (REB)

Hymn   'We sing a song of the saints of God'
             or 'For all the saints'

Prayer of thanksgiving
On this happy day, we thank you, heavenly Father, for our
church here in   .   .   .   We praise you for all the joy we have
known in this church family; for all our friends here; for leaders
and helpers; for those who plan and those who care, so that our
church may be a real home for all who share its life.
We thank you for the vision of the men and women who worked
and gave so that the church could be built, and we thank you for
all the loving sacrifice which has been shared over the years.
Help us to realize that we are one with all Christians, no matter
which church they attend, and that we are called to show the
world the joy and fullness of life which can be found only in
Jesus Christ.
May our church be a blessing to all in this neighbourhood, so
that more and more people come to love and trust you.

from *Prayers for the Church Community* (NCEC)

OUR CHURCH: Yesterday and today

Comment
*Draw attention to the frieze of the church's history (see Preparation). Use it
to tell the church's story. If possible, select two or three key times in the
history and illustrate them with dramatic interludes.*

First candle   *Invite an older person to light the first candle, saying:*
             I light a candle in thankful memory of all those who have
             served this church in the past.

Hymn   'Thanks be to God, whose Church on earth'
             or 'From glory to glory advancing'

Bible reading   Hebrews 12.1-2

SAINTS: Who are they?

Comment
What kind of people are saints? Do they have to be well known? Do
they need the 'seal of approval' of the church, fully guaranteed before

they can be called saints? Are they later candidates for a stained glass window?

The writers of the Bible didn't think so. Paul used the word 'saint' when he greeted ordinary Christians in his letters. Listen!

Arrange for four people to stand up, wherever they are in the church, and read the following extracts.

1. From Paul, an apostle of Christ Jesus by the will of God, to the church of God which is at Corinth, with all the saints who are in the whole of Achaia.

    2 Corinthians 1.1 (RSV)

2. Paul and Timothy, servants of Christ Jesus to all the saints in Christ Jesus who are at Philippi.

    Philippians 1.1 (RSV)

3. Paul, an apostle of Christ Jesus by the will of God, to the saints at Ephesus: grace to you and peace from God our Father and the Lord Jesus Christ.

    Ephesians 1.1-2 (RSV)

4. Paul, an apostle of Christ Jesus by the will of God, to the saints and faithful brethren in Christ who are at Colossae. Grace to you and peace from God our Father.

    Colossians 1.1-2 (RSV)

Comment

If Paul were writing to us, he would give us the same title. We are the saints of this generation.

An Act of Thanksgiving

Tell the congregation that a few people have been invited to nominate this year's 'saints'. Invite those previously chosen to speak their sentence from their place in the congregation, with a loud clear voice. Then ask the congregation to take the triangular pennant given to them at the beginning of the service, and write on it the names of people who have been a spiritual influence on them – they have been 'saints' for them.

It might include parents, teachers, children's workers, authors, or a friend in the congregation.

Hymn   *by choir, soloist or small singing group*
'Ubi caritas et amor'
or 'Through our lives and by our prayers'
or some other reflective song/chorus about discipleship

During the singing of the hymn, invite the congregation quietly to fasten their pennants onto the available string.

Prayer *Announce that the prayers were written by four saints. Two were well known across the world, two by local saints.*

Be thou a bright flame before me,
be thou a guiding star before me,
be thou a smooth path below me,
be thou a kindly shepherd behind me,
today, tonight and for ever.

Columba

A prayer written by a member of the congregation.

Lord, make me an instrument of your peace.
Where there is hatred, let me sow love,
where there is doubt, faith;
Where there is despair, hope;
Where there is darkness, light;
Where there is sadness, joy.
O divine Master, grant that I may not so much seek
To be consoled as to console,
To be understood as to understand,
To be loved as to love,
For it is in giving that we receive;
It is in pardoning that we are pardoned;
It is in dying that we are born to eternal life.

Francis of Assisi

A prayer written by a member of the congregation.

Story: *Choosing the harder way – a prophetic saint*

Mrs Barbara Webb didn't want any of her taxes to be spent on defence, so she sent the Inland Revenue two cheques – one for half of her tax, and the other covering the other half, but made payable to the Department of Overseas Development. Tax officials would not accept the second cheque and eventually bailiffs arrived and took away furniture to cover the debt. Typically, Mrs Webb felt sorry for the bailiff – she told him she was sorry he had such a wretched job to do.

Mrs Webb is 80. Her campaigns have been running for many years. In the Second World War she was a conscientious objector and refused to do any war work. In the sixties she took part in the Aldermaston campaigns and other demonstrations. She was arrested several times for 'sit-downs' in public places, such as Greenham.

Now she is kept busy in Portishead, where she lives, by helping in the Oxfam shop and attending Quaker gatherings at the Friends' Meeting House.

In a newspaper interview, she said, 'A lot of elderly people sit down and let the world go by, but I think that's the way to age much more quickly'. She took on the Inland Revenue because she sees a bleak future if things go on as they are. She says of her life-long rebellion, 'It's being so stubborn that has got me through all this.'

Based on an article by Quita Morgan

Second candle *Invite the four people who have prayed to step forward. One of them lights the second candle, saying:*

> We light a candle to celebrate the discipleship of all saints – past and present.

Hymn   'Brother, sister, let me serve you'
          or 'Be thou my vision'

SAINTS: Dedicated to the future

Comment

God is already preparing our future. He calls us to work with him in his mission and ministry to all people. There may be some place or some time where the contribution we each make is critically important to the purposes of God.

Meditation

> God has created me to do him some definite service. He has committed some work to me which he has not committed to another. I have my mission. I may never know it in this world, but I shall be told it in the next.
> I will trust him. Wherever, whatever I am, I can never be thrown away. If I am in sickness, my sickness may serve him; in perplexity, my perplexity may serve him; if I am in sorrow, my sorrow may serve him. God knows what he is about.

John Henry Newman (summarized)

Invite each member of the congregation to move to the nearest string of pennants and write their own name on one of the pennants. It need not be the pennant on which they wrote the name of a 'saint' who had helped them.

Hymn   'Moses, I know you're the man'
          or 'For the joys of service thee we praise'

Third candle *Invite a group of younger people (mixed ages) to step forward. One of them lights the candle, all saying:*
          We light a candle for the future of this church.

Prayer
Use several voices i.e. a teenager, a twenty/thirty year old and an older person.

TEENAGER	Lord God, we bring gifts. We bring the past of this church as a gift to you: the experience it has given us: its successes and failures, its wisdom and folly, its hurt and its remembered joy;
THREE VOICES	and with the past we bring our prayer that we may use it to understand ourselves, the people around us, and our part in the life of the world, thus enriching the work we do in your name.
TWENTY/THIRTY YEAR OLD	We bring the present as a gift to you: this fleeting moment slipping through our minds, this day in which we worship and reflect on life, this opportunity to understand and be understood, this church which serves and worships in the present moment;
THREE VOICES	and with the present we bring the prayer that we may be sensitive to your presence within it, and be thus enabled to make it a thank-offering of love.
OLDER PERSON	We bring the future to you: it is uncertainly ours, yet still it is our gift to you, it is unknown yet still we believe we can offer it in Christ's name;
THREE VOICES	and with the future we bring our visions and hopes for it, our fear and apprehension, in the confidence that, living in the eternal now, you will be our God.
LEADER	Lord God, we bring our gifts: the past, the present and the future. And yet how can we? They are already yours; your gifts to us.

40

Show us rather how to use what you have
given, rejoice in what you are giving, and
trust you for what we are yet to receive.

from *Prayers for the Church Community*

Hymn   'We sing a song of the saints of God'
or 'We are your people, Lord'
or 'We come unto our faithful (fathers') God'

*During the singing of this hymn, the three people who have lit the candles
should take one candle each and move to the ends of the rows to light the
candles of those sitting there. They in turn light their neighbour's candle
until all in the congregation hold lighted candles. The benediction then
follows.*

Benediction
Go out as lights in a dark world,
As living stones of God's house, the world.
As flowers in the wilderness.
As flags celebrating the kingdom's presence.
Be filled with courage and with joy,
Be sustained by song and sacrament,
Be guided by God's Word in Christ Jesus.
The grace of our Lord Jesus Christ,
the Love of God
and Fellowship of the Holy Spirit
be with you all, Amen

David Jenkins

Pattern using 73 hexagons refer to page 7
C. Colour hexagon   P. Pattern hexagon

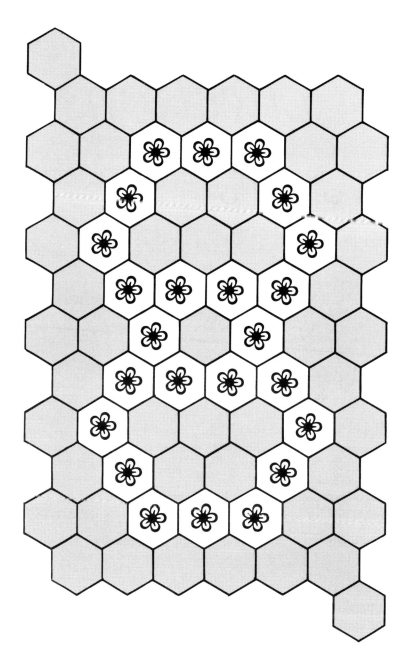

A suggested design for interlocking pattern refer to page 8

A Collection Of Collections

THE TWO MULES

A fable for the Nations

CO-OPERATION
IS BETTER THAN CONFLICT

*Available from Quaker Peace & Service, Friends House,
Euston Road, London NW1 2BJ*

ACKNOWLEDGEMENTS

The editor and publishers gratefully acknowledge permission to reproduce the following copyright material.

Every effort has been made to trace copyright holders, but if any rights have been inadvertently overlooked, the necessary correction will be made in subsequent editions. We apologise for any apparent negligence.

Kate Johnson, Anne Knighton and Stanley Mogobo:
> From *Oceans of Prayer* compiled by Maureen Edwards and Jan S Pickard. (NCEC).

John Hunt:
> From *The Ascent of Everest* (Hodder and Stoughton Ltd).

Bernard Thorogood:
> From *Everyday Prayers* (International Bible Reading Association 1978).

John Bell and Graham Maule:
> From *Wild Goose Prints No. 3* (Wild Goose Publications)
> Copyright Iona Community, Glasgow, used by permission.

Edmund Banyard:
> From *Turn But a Stone* (NCEC).

David Jenkins (adapted):
> From *Further Everyday Prayers* (NCEC).

Kurt Kauter:
> From *New Fables*, 'Thus Spoke the Marabou'.

Items from Prayers for the *Church Community* (NCEC).

Quita Morgan:
> From *The Bristol Evening Post* 8/10/86 and quoted in *Partners in Learning 1988* (NCEC/MDEY).

'Two mules' poster (Quaker Peace and Service) used by permission.

We are grateful for permission to quote from the following versions of the Bible:

REB   *The Revised English Bible* (© 1989 Oxford and Cambridge University Presses).

RSV   *The Bible Revised Standard Version* © 1989 Division of Christian Education of the National Council of the Churches of Christ in the United States of America).

MORE RESOURCES FOR ALL AGE WORSHIP FROM NCEC

CELEBRATING SERIES

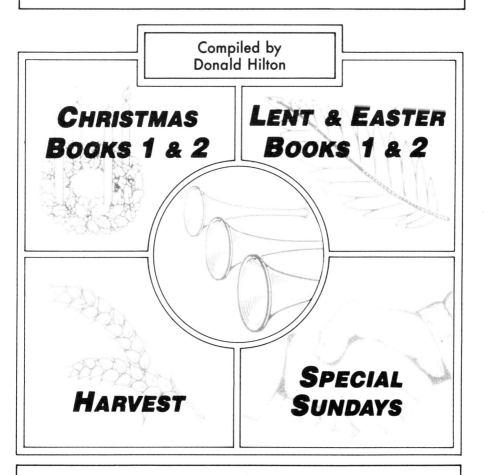

Compiled by
Donald Hilton

CHRISTMAS BOOKS 1 & 2

LENT & EASTER BOOKS 1 & 2

HARVEST

SPECIAL SUNDAYS

FESTIVAL SERVICES for the Church Year

Sold individually or in a set with a substantial saving

Available from all good Christian bookshops or, in case of difficulty, from NCEC direct.

Other Titles from RADIUS and NCEC

THE HILL
Sylvia Read
0-7197-0761-7

A modern mystery play in which the characters find themselves caught up in the experience of Easter. 30 mins.

Code No. PLA0761 (A)

CROSSTALK
Bob Irving
0-7197-0795-1

A collection of ten short plays based upon the parables which were, in their own time, sharp contemporary stories in an established tradition. In order to convey the same sense of immediacy these sketches are presented in a highly modern quick firing style. No need for props or costumes, maximum cast of five. Each play lasts about 5 minutes.

Code No. PLA0795 (A)

SURPRISE SKETCHES
Ronald Rich
0-7197-0796-X

Five one-act plays with surprising endings. Ideal as a prompter for discussion or for use in worship, these plays examine some familiar human failings in a new stimulating style. Each play runs for about 10 minutes.

Code No. PLA0796 (A)

THE FLAME
Edmund Banyard
0-7197-0709-9

A novel approach to the idea of Pentecost, this play is a one act fantasy in the style of the Theatre of the Absurd. Four ordinary people are offered the 'Light of the World' by a messenger from the border between Time and Eternity. 25 mins.

Code No. FLA0709 (A)

> Performance times given are
> very approximate.

A FISTFUL OF FIVERS
Edmund Banyard
0-7197-0667-X

Twelve five-minute plays, each with a Christian message. Using the minimum of actors, scenery and props, these lively sketches will appeal to everyone who is young in the widest sense.

Code No. PLA0667 (A)

A FUNNY THING HAPPENED ON THE WAY TO JERICHO
Tom Long
0-7197-0722-6

The dress rehearsal for a presentation of the Good Samaritan turns out to be more than the leading player intended, as she is challenged by each of the roles she takes on in her search for the one she feels happy with. 30 mins.

Code No. FUN0722 (A) R

THE PRODIGAL DAUGHTER
William Fry
0-7197-0668-8

Using a neat twist, William Fry has turned one of the best-known parables into the tale of a present-day girl, updating the setting to portray some of the concerns of modern society. While it shows the seamier side of contemporary life, the message of this play is ultimately one of redemption and love. 30 mins.

Code No. PLA0668 (A)

NATIVITY LETTERS
Nick Warburton
0-7197-0724-2

Highlights the strains put on mother and daughter in the interdependence of a single parent family, which make them tend to disassociate themselves from other people. Help eventually presents itself through a committed teacher in the daughter's drama group. 40 mins.

Code No. NAT0724 (A)

WHO'LL BE BROTHER DONKEY?
Arthur Scholey
0-7197-0723-4

Three traditional Christmas tales are combined to produce this play where the animals use their Christmas Eve gift of speech to enact the crib scene in the hillside chapel. During the journey from their stable they outwit the wily Fox and Vixen in their malevolent schemes. The conclusion shows how the preparation of the crib scene is achieved against all odds through forgiveness of their fellow creatures and faith. 60 mins.

Code No. WHO0723 (A)